W9-AUB-607

GRADES 4–8

The Essential Questions Handbook

New York • Toronto • London • Auckland • Sydney
Mexico City • New Delhi • Hong Kong • Buenos Aires

Teaching Resources

Picture Credits

8 Robertlamphoto/Shutterstock; 10 Jiawangkun/Shutterstock; 12 Asc/Shutterstock; 14 Nagel Photography/Shutterstock; 16 Bull's-Eye Arts/Shutterstock; 18 Holger W./Shutterstock; 20 Racheal Grazias/Shutterstock; 22 Philip Eckerberg/Shutterstock; 24 Dwight Nadig/Istockphoto; 26 Paul Hakimata Photography/Shutterstock; 28 Everett Collection/Rex Feature; 30 JPL/NASA; 32 NASA; 34 Smit/Shutterstock; 36 Mike Phillips/Shutterstock; 38 Clm/Shutterstock; 40 Beltsazar/Shutterstock; 42 Robyn Waserman/National Science Foundation/United States Antarctic Program; 44 Maksimilian/Shutterstock; 46 Jupiterimages/Photos.com/Thinkstock; 48 Niar/Shutterstock; 50 Nina Shannon/Istockphoto; 53 Forster Forest/Shutterstock; 58 Kapu/Shutterstock; 60 Arlo K. Abrahamson/U.S. Navy; 62 Jupiterimages/Brand X Pictures/Thinkstock; 64 Wolfson, Stanley/Library of Congress; 66 Brenda Bailey/Shutterstock; 68 Iafoto/Shutterstock; 70 Clive Watkins/Shutterstock; 72 Ocsi Balazs/Shutterstock; 74 Gemphotography/Shutterstock; 76 Todd Taulman/Shutterstock; 78 Alejandro Rivera/Istockphoto; 80 Mythja/Shutterstock; 82 Sculpies/Shutterstock; 84 Africa Studio/Shutterstock; 86 Haywiremedia/Shutterstock

Written by Carolyn McConnell
Cover design by Brian LaRossa
Interior design and production by Q2A Media

Copyright © 2011 by Q2A Media. All rights reserved. Published by Scholastic Inc.
Printed in the U.S.A.

ISBN: 978-0-545-30585-3

3 4 5 6 7 8 9 10   40   17 16 15 14 13

Contents

Big Ideas, Big Questions

Learning starts when students start thinking. Lessons that work well require two key ingredients: ideas worth thinking about and hooks to lead students to dig in and think. Great questions make great hooks.

The best questions for stimulating student thinking are the ones that cannot be answered easily. In fact, the best questions often have no answer—at least, no one "correct" answer. Such questions are called **essential questions,** and they are at the heart of every discipline.

But what exactly are essential questions? How do they differ from the questions often posed at the end of a lesson, or the ones that show up on a test? Here are some characteristics.

? Essential Questions

- **Focus on ideas that matter to us, and that we have a desire or need to understand.**
- **Get to the heart of a discipline and lead to "enduring understandings"—core concepts that can be applied to other problems and situations.**
- **Have no one "right" answer; instead, they result in different points of view and opinions.**
- **Do not have answers that can be found in books or online; the answers must be invented, concluded, or imagined.**
- **Engage students in real-life problem solving.**
- **Usually have meaning and applications across several disciplines.**
- **Get asked and re-asked over time, leading to answers that are increasingly sophisticated.**
- **Are framed to engage students and maintain their interest; they are thought-provoking, intriguing, even exciting. Students feel compelled to answer them.**
- **Are accessible to all students, no matter what their interests or learning styles. Good essential questions provide a common ground for discussion, irrespective of ability level or background.**
- **Lead naturally to other questions that students generate to clarify ideas or push the exploration forward.**
- **Can take a lifetime to answer!**

What are essential questions about?
What matters most!

Any unit of study in any curriculum includes multiple facts, skills, and understandings. At the heart of a unit will be the most important learnings that students should remember in a year—and in a lifetime. These critical insights that students need to retain after they have forgotten smaller details are the "enduring understandings." They are core statements, generalizations about the big ideas. They are the important understandings that will anchor a unit of study.

Enduring Understandings

- Focus on the overarching concepts that matter most
- Have lasting value
- Are at the heart of a discipline
- Can transfer to new situations
- Relate to the real world

Essential questions help students come to grips with the enduring understandings. They point students in a direction and give them reasons to think and to investigate the key facets of any enduring understandings. Essential questions spark inquiry that will lead students to their own questions, and they ensure that students will climb the ladder of critical-thinking skills. Essential questions require students to

- Explore, explain, and analyze
- Interpret
- Examine from several points of view
- Synthesize
- Apply understandings to new situations

Using Best Practices

Year after year, teachers ask their own essential question: What are the best practices and methods for engaging and teaching students? By strategically planning lessons around enduring understandings and essential questions, teachers can help address issues of motivation, effective use of class time, long-term retention, differentiation, cross-curricular connections, and critical thinking.

Each lesson planning guide—

- Centers learning around "big-picture" content worth remembering for life
- Provides focus and direction to attain mastery of key standards
- Gives students a reason to engage, inquire, research, and question
- Supplies authentic reasons for students to sharpen their literacy skills
- Helps students relate important ideas to their own lives
- Leads students to connect understandings across the curriculum
- Ensures that students practice analyzing, synthesizing, and evaluating
- Establishes learning goals that use time well
- Enables students to transfer learning to new situations and contexts

How to Begin

The purpose of this book is to provide a ready supply of carefully crafted enduring understandings and essential questions. They are the starting points for planning motivating, effective units of study built around key curriculum-based big ideas.

The pages that follow are divided into subject areas: social studies, science, language arts, and mathematics. For each subject area, you will find a selection of "big ideas"—concepts that are crucial to understanding the subject area at the upper-elementary grade levels. You will recognize the social studies, science, and math concepts as key focuses in your state standards. For language arts, you will find both an array of thematic big ideas that students will encounter in their reading and literature selections and big ideas about approaches to reading genre-specific literature.

Each two-page planning guide provides

- A Big Idea—Curricular focus for study of a concept
- Enduring Understandings—Key learning goals built around the big idea
- Vocabulary List—Subject area words that students may encounter and use in their explorations
- Essential Questions—A menu of starting points that lead students to explore and think deeply about the topic

Tips for Planning

- Choose the big ideas that fit your curriculum needs.
- Choose two to five essential questions that best fit your unit plan and your students' needs.
- Design concrete exploratory activities for each question.
- Decide ahead what assessments and performance tasks you will use that directly link to the essential questions.
- Post the essential questions in the classroom.
- Encourage students to bring in any sort of evidence, stories, etc., that helps them connect the questions to their own lives.

Planning Integrated Units of Study

A focus on big ideas is the ideal starting point for planning integrated units of study across several content areas. The final section of the book provides models for using the big ideas in this book as the basis for planning integrated units of study across several areas of the curriculum. These models are suggested starting points and can be adapted to fit individual needs and resources.

Community

The concept of community appears in almost every aspect of the natural world. It refers to neighborhoods and cities created by people, but it also describes a pride of lions or a pod of whales. It provides a context for stories in literature, explains ecosystems in nature, drives politics and culture, and offers security and structure to individuals in their everyday lives.

Enduring Understandings

- There are different types of communities: physical/social, human/animal, and formal/informal.

- A community is made up of individuals.

- Every individual in a community has a role and responsibility.

- Relationships and interdependencies develop within a community.

- Within a community, we encounter and should respect alternative viewpoints and values.

- Communities are strongest when people take active roles in maintaining them.

Vocabulary List

- Conflict
- Cooperation
- Global
- Interaction
- Interdependence

- Local
- Municipal
- Mutual
- Organization
- Perspective

- Relationship
- Respect
- Social
- Tolerance

Essential Questions

Use these questions to guide student exploration of the concept of community.

- What makes a community?

- Why do people form communities?

- What does a community need to survive?

- What is an individual's responsibility to a community? What is the community's responsibility to each individual?

- How important are honesty and fairness in a community?

- How important are laws in maintaining a community?

- How important is it to belong to a community?

- Is every community a physical place?

Add your own questions!

Big Idea 2

Government

The study of the concept of government allows students to understand the development of structures of power for maintaining order in societies. This foundation is important for helping students understand and appreciate the unique characteristics of American representational democracy.

Enduring Understandings

- Governments exist to provide order and services to a nation.

- People create governments to help control conflict and maintain order.

- Each government has its own unique power and structure.

- Forms of government can change over time.

- Conflict can change the way citizens act in a government.

- A democracy is a form of government that represents the people, protects rights, and helps determine the common good.

Vocabulary List

- Authority
- Congress
- Democracy
- Dictatorship
- Federal

- Majority
- Minority
- Monarchy
- National
- Political

- Power
- Representative
- Republic
- System

Essential Questions

Use these questions to stimulate student thinking about the role of government and laws in society.

- What is power and where does power to govern come from?

- How do governments get and use power?

- For what purposes do governments exist?

- How are governments created and structured?

- How are governments maintained and changed?

- What does a government need to do to survive?

- How do different types of government affect the people who live under each system?

- What does it mean to live in a democracy?

- How is a government useful to its citizens?

- Why do we need laws?

- What impact can citizens have on their government?

- What would happen if we had no government?

Add your own questions!

The Constitution

The United States Constitution embodies the American values of self-government, distributed powers, and individual freedoms. How it came to be, the type of government it provides, how it continues to sustain a powerful nation, and how it serves as a model for others are important aspects worth exploring.

Enduring Understandings

- The constitution of a nation is a document that provides organization and structure for its government.

- The constitutions of democratic governments describe the rights and responsibilities of citizens.

- The Constitution of the United States is a living document that helps define the roles and responsibilities of the government.

- The Constitution establishes a government of limited powers shared among different branches of government.

- The Constitution provides a strong guarantee of the rights of citizens.

- The Constitution and the Bill of Rights have created a successful government that has been a model for other countries.

Vocabulary List

- Amendment
- Bill of Rights
- Branches of government
- Checks and balances
- Executive
- House of Representatives
- Judicial
- Legislative
- Liberty
- Preamble
- Senate
- Separation of powers
- Supreme Court
- Unalienable

Essential Questions

Use these questions to guide student exploration of the United States Constitution.

- What drives people to seek independence?

- What steps did colonists take to form a government?

- How does the U.S. Constitution reflect the people and times it came from?

- What beliefs about democracy are expressed in the Constitution?

- How does the Constitution provide for the rights of citizens?

- Why does the Constitution separate the powers of government?

- What key powers does each branch have?

- What is meant by "checks and balances"?

- Why do we have a Bill of Rights?

- Why do human rights need to be protected?

- Why is the Preamble to the Constitution important?

- Why can the Constitution be called a "living document"?

- Why might another country want to copy the United States Constitution?

Add your own questions!

Big Idea 4

Citizenship

A healthy democracy depends on the education and participation of its citizens. Social studies curricula include the vital task of helping students acquire the understandings, skills, and attitudes they will need to be educated participants. Supporting students in thinking critically about the roles and responsibilities of citizenship is an important part of that task.

Enduring Understandings

- Rules and laws set up the relationship between a government and its citizens.

- With citizenship comes roles, rights, and responsibilities.

- In a democracy, citizenship requires active, lifelong participation.

- The rights of citizens may be protected by a constitution.

- Citizens can influence the way that government works.

- Citizens contribute to the lives of others by doing something for the community.

Vocabulary List

- Allegiance
- Ballot
- Campaign
- Civic-minded
- Common good
- Consent
- Election
- Obligation
- Participatory
- Patriotism
- Political party
- Register
- Responsibilities
- Rights

Essential Questions

Use these questions for students to explore the privileges and responsibilities of citizenship.

- What is citizenship?

- What are the roles and responsibilities of a citizen in the community and in the nation?

- Why does good citizenship matter in a democracy?

- How can Americans be good citizens?

- Why is liberty important to citizens?

- What are the qualities of a responsible citizen?

- How does being a good citizen affect others?

- Why is being an informed voter important in a democracy?

- Why is public service important in a democracy?

- How do citizens make their voices heard?

- How do citizens show patriotism?

- How can students in elementary school be good citizens?

- What does it mean to be a citizen in a global community?

Add your own questions!

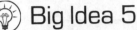

Big Idea 5

Native Americans

The study of Native Americans is ideal for helping students deepen their understanding of the factors that cause a culture to emerge, grow, and change. It can also lead to a deepening appreciation for Native Americans' varied histories and cultural contributions. Student exploration can be customized to focus on particular local groups of Native Americans if the curriculum specifies.

Enduring Understandings

- The search for resources can cause groups of people to move.

- Geography influences the movement and interaction of different cultural groups.

- The natural resources of a region affect the types of food, clothing, shelter, transportation, and tools that people create.

- All cultures are unique; cultures share similarities and differences.

- Native Americans established successful cultures in North America.

- Relations between cultures can mean both conflict and cooperation.

Vocabulary List

- Agriculture
- Ancestor
- Artifact
- Cultural heritage
- Diversity

- Environment
- Ethnic group
- Indigenous
- Land bridge
- Legend

- Migration
- Natural resource
- Oral tradition
- Tribal

Essential Questions

Use these questions to explore the many facets of Native American cultures.

- Why did people first migrate to the Americas?

- How did Native Americans adapt to their environments?

- Why did Native American cultures differ across North America?

- What are similarities and differences in the ways groups of Native Americans met their needs?

- How did environments influence the items Native Americans created?

- What characteristics are often unique to a group's identity?

- What do stories, legends, and art tell about the culture of the Native Americans who created them?

- How did Native Americans interact with Europeans who arrived?

- What were causes of conflict between Native American groups and other settlers?

- How have Native Americans affected the history of the United States?

- How did the way of life of Native Americans change over time?

- How are Native American traditions kept alive?

Add your own questions!

Age of Exploration

Events, ideas, and discoveries from the Renaissance resulted in the European Age of Exploration from 1400 to 1600. Curiosity and religious fervor, combined with a desire to find new trade routes, goods, and resources, led to Europeans' encounters with previously unknown native peoples. The cultural interactions that resulted forever altered the course of history.

 Enduring Understandings

- European countries had many reasons to send explorers to new lands.

- Explorers changed Europeans' views of the world.

- Trade, cultural exchanges, and conflict can result when explorers reach new lands.

- The Age of Exploration had positive and negative effects on Europeans and on native peoples.

- Exploration has had a profound effect on world history.

- Events in history can be looked at from multiple perspectives.

Vocabulary List

- Astrolabe
- Circumnavigate
- Colony
- Columbian exchange
- Compass

- Conquistador
- Empire
- Expedition
- Latitude
- Longitude

- Navigation
- Northwest Passage
- Renaissance
- Smallpox

Essential Questions

Use these questions to help students think further about the concept of exploration.

- Why are explorers important in history?

- What caused the Age of Exploration?

- What ideas and discoveries made exploration possible?

- Why did certain individuals want to become explorers?

- What are some things explorers did in the new lands?

- What problems did European explorers face?

- What were the effects of exploration on Europe, Africa, and the Americas?

- How did explorers contribute to people's knowledge of the world?

- Which explorers have had the greatest effect on history?

- What were the similarities and differences between the native peoples and the Europeans?

- How did exploration affect the lives of native people?

- Why is the Age of Exploration considered a turning point in history?

Add your own questions!

American Revolution

The study of the American Revolution can help students understand how events in history can have complex causes and both immediate and long-term effects. It also allows opportunities to focus on the roles of individuals in history and on the importance of key historical documents such as the Declaration of Independence.

 ## Enduring Understandings

- Ideas can cause change.

- Change comes out of revolutions.

- Conflicts can stem from multiple causes and can have multiple results.

- The events of the American Revolution were influenced by several events that came before it.

- The colonists disagreed with the British over the proper relationship between government and citizens.

- A new nation was created as a result of the American Revolution.

- Individuals can have a great impact on history.

Vocabulary List

- Boston Massacre
- Boston Tea Party
- Boycott
- Colonist
- Continental Congress
- Declaration of Independence
- Loyalist
- Mercenary
- Militia
- Minuteman
- Patriot
- Redcoat
- Taxation without representation

Essential Questions

Use these questions to build on any prior knowledge students may have about the American Revolution.

- How does conflict create change?

- What is independence?

- Why was there an American Revolution?

- What made the American Revolution revolutionary?

- How did ideas cause the American Revolution?

- Why was the Declaration of Independence important?

- What role did geography play for the armies on both sides?

- How were the colonists able to defeat the British army?

- What other ways could the colonists and the British Parliament have solved their problems?

- How can we look at the American Revolution from different points of view?

- What were the immediate and long-term results of the American Revolution?

- Why was the American Revolution an important event in world history?

Add your own questions!

Big Idea 8

Westward Expansion

In the nineteenth century, the United States exploded in size and population due to westward expansion. Pioneers went west for a variety of reasons, and Native American cultures were drastically affected. The Lewis and Clark expedition, the Gold Rush, the Oregon Trail, the Homestead Act, and the transcontinental railroad all contributed to changing the face of America.

 Enduring Understandings

- People move for a variety of reasons.

- In the 1800s, the United States underwent a tremendous amount of exploration, expansion, and settlement of lands west of the Mississippi River.

- Westward expansion was influenced by geography and economic opportunity.

- Successful pioneers used collaboration, courage, and imagination to overcome challenges.

- Change and progress can have both positive and negative effects.

- Westward expansion forever altered the lives of Native Americans.

Vocabulary List

- Annex
- Boundary
- Conestoga wagon
- Forty-niner
- Frontier
- Great Plains
- Homesteader
- Homestead Act
- Louisiana Purchase
- Nationalism
- Oregon Trail
- Pioneer
- Squatter
- Transcontinental

Essential Questions

Use these questions to help students understand the issues leading to and resulting from westward expansion.

- Why did pioneers move from the East to the western frontier in the nineteenth century?

- What challenges did they face on their journeys?

- Why do people take risks like those experienced during westward expansion?

- What role did the American government play in the movement westward?

- Why was the Lewis and Clark expedition important?

- What challenges did pioneers who settled in western lands face?

- Why did some pioneers prosper, and why did others not prosper?

- What is the "pioneer spirit"?

- How did westward expansion affect Native Americans, then and now?

- How did technology affect westward expansion?

- How did westward expansion change the American economy?

Add your own questions!

Civil War

The Civil War was a pivotal event in American history and has fascinated and captured people's imagination ever since. Because of it, the union of states was saved, slavery was ended, new ways of waging war were pioneered, new types of journalism appeared, fortunes were made and lost, and more American lives were lost than in any war since. It is also a great lens for studying how war affects a society geographically, economically, politically, and socially.

Enduring Understandings

- Beliefs can influence actions.

- Social and economic problems can divide a nation and lead to war.

- Conflicts in a society can lead to changes, both positive and negative.

- A civil war creates long-lasting divisions within a country.

- Leaders can have great influence on events.

- Ending slavery did not end the effects of slavery.

Vocabulary List

- Abolition
- Assassination
- Border state
- Casualty
- Confederacy

- Cotton gin
- Emancipation Proclamation
- Gettysburg Address
- Plantation
- Reconstruction

- Secession
- Sectionalism
- States' rights
- Underground railroad
- Union

Essential Questions

Use these questions to help students examine the causes and effects of the Civil War.

- Do wars have to be fought?

- What effects can a civil war have on a nation?

- How was the way of life in the South different from life in the North?

- Why was the Civil War fought?

- What part did slavery play in the Civil War?

- Was the Civil War avoidable?

- What events in the Civil War made the most difference in the outcome?

- What role did Abraham Lincoln play in the war?

- What role did African Americans play in bringing about their own emancipation?

- How did Americans rebuild after the Civil War?

- What were the costs of the Civil War?

- Why is the Civil War so important in American history?

- How did the Civil War change the United States?

Add your own questions!

Big Idea 10

Immigration

Throughout history, people have made the decision to uproot their lives and move to a new country. Those who have the courage to leave familiar surroundings face a variety of challenges and conflicts as they resettle. However, they also bring their cultural heritage, which can enrich their new societies. History and literature are filled with stories about the immigrant experience. Many students can themselves relate first- and second-hand accounts of immigration in their own families.

Enduring Understandings

- People move to new lands for many reasons.

- Many factors influence where immigrants will live in the new lands.

- Immigrants face challenges in their new surroundings.

- Conflicts can arise over immigration.

- Immigrants maintain old traditions and develop new traditions.

- Immigrants make contributions to their new cultures.

Vocabulary List

- Assimilate
- Contribution
- Deportation
- Detention center
- Ellis Island

- Emigration
- Ethnic
- Influx
- Naturalization
- Origin

- Policy
- Push-pull factors
- Quarantine
- Quota

Essential Questions

Use these questions to guide student inquiry into the big idea of immigration.

- Why do people leave their homelands and move to new places?

- What factors might someone think about before deciding to immigrate?

- What challenges do immigrants face in their new homes?

- What makes immigration easier for some and harder for others?

- How can immigration lead to conflict?

- How do immigrants contribute to their new countries?

- What factors influence an immigrant's chance of success in a new country?

- What causes some citizens to make immigrants feel unwelcome?

- Why might citizens have different viewpoints on immigration?

- How has immigration shaped our nation?

- Do people migrate today for the same reasons as in the past?

- Is America still a land of opportunity for immigrants?

Add your own questions!

Big Idea 11

Civil Rights Movement

During the historic Civil Rights movement of the 1950s and 1960s, African Americans strengthened efforts to achieve their rights. They used a variety of strategies to address discrimination and inequality in areas such as education, housing, employment, and voting. The Civil Rights movement inspired similar efforts in many places throughout the world.

 Enduring Understandings

- Denying human rights leads to oppression.

- Individuals and groups can bring about change in society through social action.

- Societies react to change in a variety of ways.

- Changing the law does not always change peoples' attitudes.

- The Civil Rights movement furthered the promises of equality for all citizens.

- The struggle for equality still goes on.

Vocabulary List

- Activist
- Boycott
- Busing
- Civil liberties
- Desegregation

- Discrimination
- Freedom rider
- Integration
- Jim Crow Laws
- Militant

- Nonviolent resistance
- Racism
- "Separate but equal"
- Sit-in

Essential Questions

Use these questions to help students understand the historic struggles and achievements of the Civil Rights movement.

- What were the origins of the Civil Rights movement of the 1950s and 1960s?

- Can separate be equal?

- What goals did the Civil Rights movement strive for?

- How did different groups achieve change in the Civil Rights movement?

- How did court cases affect the Civil Rights movement?

- What is the responsibility of those with rights toward those deprived of rights?

- What was Martin Luther King, Jr.'s, impact on the Civil Rights movement?

- How do changes in laws change peoples' attitudes?

- What overall effect did the Civil Rights movement have?

- Why does racial prejudice still exist?

- How is the struggle for rights in America related to struggles for rights worldwide?

Add your own questions!

Solar System

Our vast solar system is a collection of interacting bodies that behave according to the principles of gravity. Forces at work in the solar system account for the patterns that we take for granted in everyday life, such as day and night, tides, and seasons of the year. The solar system remains a frontier to be explored. Uncovering even more of its secrets will require advances in technology and the imaginations of dreamers.

Enduring Understandings

- Systems have cycles and patterns that allow us to make predictions.

- There are observable, predictable patterns of movement in the solar system.

- The sun is a star that drives Earth's systems and is essential for life.

- Stars form and change over time.

- Physical characteristics of planets depend on their size and distance from the sun.

- Humans study and explore the sun, moon, and planets to learn about their past, present, and future history.

Vocabulary List

- Alignment
- Asteroid
- Axis
- Comet
- Constellation
- Eclipse
- Galaxy
- Gravity
- Lunar
- Meteorite
- Orbit
- Phases
- Planet
- Rotation
- Satellite

Essential Questions

Use these questions to help guide student exploration into our solar system.

- How can patterns be used to describe the universe?

- Why is our solar system a system?

- How is our solar system organized?

- How does the sun affect the other planets?

- What is the role of gravity in the solar system?

- What adaptations would you have to make to live on another planet?

- What accounts for day and night, seasons, months, and tides?

- How is our knowledge of the solar system affected by technology?

- How could people in the past think that Earth was the center of the solar system?

- Why do humans explore the solar system?

- Why was landing on the moon a great achievement?

- How can studying the solar system lead to a better Earth?

Add your own questions!

Planet Earth

In 1972, the crew of the spaceship Apollo 17 took a photograph that changed how people view their home planet Earth. The photo sparked renewed interest in and study of the planet—a complex system of interacting components that includes air, land, water, and life. Today, we know that an understanding of how Earth works can help us better appreciate and maintain its dynamic beauty.

Enduring Understandings

- Systems interact and influence each other.

- Earth is part of a system of planets that orbit the sun.

- Earth is a system of systems.

- Earth's surface, atmosphere, and life are constantly changing due to internal and external forces.

- Processes that shape Earth can be helpful, harmful, or both.

- Humans depend on and modify Earth's resources and systems.

Vocabulary List

- Atmosphere
- Biosphere
- Composition
- Crust
- Dynamic
- Earthquake
- Fault
- Geography
- Global warming
- Hydrosphere
- Lithosphere
- Mantle
- Ozone
- Plate tectonics
- Surface

Essential Questions

Use these questions to kindle students' curiosity about their home planet.

- Why should we recognize patterns that exist in our world?

- How does planet Earth function within the solar system?

- How does Earth change?

- How are Earth's systems connected?

- How is life on Earth affected by the solar system?

- Why is it important to understand Earth's systems?

- What makes our planet unique?

- What do we know about how Earth's features are formed?

- How do the processes that shape Earth affect our lives?

- What role does Earth's atmosphere play in supporting life on Earth?

- What influence do humans have on Earth's atmosphere?

- Can humans survive and thrive without using up the resources of the planet?

Add your own questions!

Water Cycle

Life on Earth is directly tied to the unique abundance of water on our planet. A never-ending cycle, fueled by energy from the sun, connects the oceans, the atmosphere, and the land, providing us with this vital resource. The water cycle is also responsible for the various climates of the world. Maintaining the health of this cycle will impact the future of all of us.

Enduring Understandings

- Water is essential for life on Earth.

- Cycles produce constant change on Earth.

- Some events in nature have a repeating pattern.

- Water plays a major role in shaping Earth's surface.

- Natural resources can be affected by human interaction.

- Local actions can have global effects.

Vocabulary List

- Aquifer
- Circulate
- Condensation
- Conserve
- Evaporation
- Glacier
- Groundwater
- Infiltration
- Precipitation
- Runoff
- Salinity
- Sublimation
- Transpiration
- Water vapor
- Watershed

Essential Questions

Use these questions to immerse students in the exploration of the water cycle.

- Why is water essential for sustaining life on Earth?

- How do we get the water we use every day?

- What are ways that water moves and changes?

- How does the water cycle impact the environment?

- How does water shape our planet?

- How does peoples' use of water affect the environment?

- Why is the water cycle important?

- What is our role in the water cycle?

- Why does the quality of water in rivers and streams matter?

- How can a local action have a global effect?

- Why is it important to learn about water?

- How would life be different if there were no water cycle?

Add your own questions!

Big Idea 15

Patterns of Weather

The study of weather is ideal for reinforcing the big ideas of systems and patterns in nature and for demonstrating the interconnectedness of these systems. It also presents an opportunity for demonstrating how scientists use technology, tools, models, and mathematics to collect and study data. Because all students come with personal experience to share about weather, its study can be quite captivating and relevant.

Enduring Understandings

- Systems have cycles and patterns.

- Patterns can be studied and used to make predictions.

- Tools help us collect data.

- Weather is a powerful force of nature.

- Weather affects all life on Earth.

- Changes in weather affect our daily lives.

Vocabulary List

- Air pressure
- Anemometer
- Barometer
- Celsius thermometer
- Climate

- Dew point
- Forecast
- Humidity
- Meteorology
- Moisture

- Pattern
- Seasons
- Temperature
- Trend
- Unstable

Essential Questions

Use these questions to help students begin building on and questioning their own insights about weather.

- How do changes in one part of Earth's systems affect other parts?

- Why is weather a system?

- How does geography play a role in natural events?

- How is weather related to water?

- How do we determine weather patterns?

- How can we use weather patterns to help explain our world?

- How can weather be described?

- How do tools help us collect data?

- How are living things affected by weather?

- Why are weather predictions not always right?

- How do humans impact weather systems on Earth?

Add your own questions!

Rocks and Minerals

A key feature of dynamic Earth is the cycle that forms and reforms the rocks and minerals that are useful to people. Students' imaginations can be captured by the study of rocks and minerals, such as the history of Earth revealed by rocks and minerals, the various ways people put them to use, the conflicts involved in obtaining them, and the challenges of their limited supply. Students can also see science at work in the tools and methods used to study and classify them.

Enduring Understandings

- The natural world is composed of interdependent systems.

- Earth's materials undergo change over varying lengths of time.

- Earth's materials have physical and chemical characteristics.

- Scientists classify and organize living and nonliving things in categories to better understand them and their relationships.

- Rocks and minerals have characteristics that make them useful to people.

- Earth's resources are limited.

Vocabulary List

- Crystalline
- Fossil
- Gemstone
- Geology
- Igneous
- Lava
- Luster
- Magma
- Metamorphic
- Mining
- Mohs Scale
- Rock cycle
- Sedentary
- Weathering

Essential Questions

Use these questions to enable students to see familiar objects in nature in new and interesting ways.

- How does Earth's surface change?

- What is Earth made of?

- How can people tell what has happened to Earth?

- How do materials cycle through systems?

- Where do rocks and minerals come from?

- Why do rocks look different from each other?

- Are the rocks we see the same ones that dinosaurs saw? Why or why not?

- What story of Earth's history can rocks and minerals tell us?

- Why are some rocks and minerals valuable to people while others are not?

- How are scientists able to sort and identify rocks?

- Why should we be concerned with studying rocks?

- How does the use of Earth's resources affect our environment?

Add your own questions!

Life Cycles

From frogs to flowers to friends, interest in living things comes naturally to students. Exploring the concept of the life cycles of living organisms is a powerful tool for helping students make sense of the complexity, diversity, and interconnectedness of life on Earth. It is also an opportunity to see order in the natural world and to see how that order can be studied and predicted using the tools of science.

Enduring Understandings

- Patterns exist in the universe.

- All living things have characteristics in common.

- There is a sequence of events in a natural cycle.

- All living things have a life cycle.

- Living things change throughout their lifetimes.

- Living organisms have identifiable features that allow them to survive as a species.

Vocabulary List

- Adaptation
- Biology
- Botany
- Cell
- Cycle

- Development
- Diversity
- Genetic
- Life cycle
- Organism

- Population
- Reproduce
- Species
- Stage
- Sustain

Essential Questions

Use these questions to help students understand the role of cycles and patterns of life on Earth.

- What are some of the cycles that occur in nature?

- What does it mean to be alive?

- What do all living things have in common?

- What are the basic needs of living things?

- What are the basic functions of living things?

- Why are living things so different yet alike?

- How do organisms change as they go through their life cycles?

- Why do organisms change over time?

- What patterns of change can be seen among organisms?

- How do individual differences occur within species of living things?

- Why is there so much diversity among living things?

Add your own questions!

Adaptation

Understanding the kinds of changes animals and plants undergo over time as a reaction to change in their environment can help students see the range of physical features, characteristics, and behaviors in nature in new and informed ways. These new insights can lead to a deepened interest in the natural world and in the study of science.

Enduring Understandings

- Living things exhibit patterns of behavior in their structures, behaviors, and chemical makeup.

- Living things interact with their environments.

- All living organisms have identifiable characteristics or traits that allow for survival.

- An organism's structure helps it survive.

- Organisms of the same kind differ in their individual characteristics or traits.

Vocabulary List

- Camouflage
- Characteristic
- Evolve
- Food chain
- Heredity

- Instinct
- Invasive
- Mimicry
- Mutation
- Natural selection

- Predator
- Protection
- Survival
- Trait
- Variation

Essential Questions

Use these questions to generate interest in the big idea of adaptation.

- What do living things need to survive?

- How is the physical makeup of a living thing related to the way it behaves?

- How does the structure of an organism help it to survive?

- How do organisms survive in harsh or hostile environments?

- How do organisms depend on one another?

- How can organisms increase their chances of survival?

- How do plants and animals adapt to their habitats?

- How do adaptations sustain life?

- What changes in environment could result in an adaptation by a living thing?

- Why are there so many different kinds of plants and animals on Earth?

- What might happen if you introduce a new species to an environment?

- How can human behavior affect plant and animal behavior?

Add your own questions!

Habitats

The study of habitats can take students from their own backyards to the frozen tundra of the Arctic, from local parks to tropical rainforests. It can also help students appreciate the diversity of the natural world, the delicate balances at work in that world, the causes and effects of change in habitats, and the role of humans in affecting the environments near and far.

Enduring Understandings

- Change can have good and bad effects.

- All living things exist in environments called habitats.

- Habitats provide basic needs for organisms.

- Living things depend on one another and on their environments.

- Environments influence the survival of living things.

- Human activity can affect environments.

Vocabulary List

- Biome
- Desert
- Ecosystem
- Environment
- Food chain

- Forest
- Grassland
- Prairie
- Rainforest
- Savanna

- Swamp
- Temperate
- Tropical
- Tundra
- Wetland

Essential Questions

Use these questions to build students' interest in the variety of environments that creatures on Earth call home.

- How are living things connected?

- Why would a scientist say, "There's no place like home"?

- Why do living things exist in different types of environments or habitats?

- How does our habitat affect the way we live?

- How are all habitats alike and different?

- What can threaten a habitat?

- How does an animal's habitat affect its survival?

- What causes conflict between human and animal habitats?

- What is the relationship between habitats and adaptations?

- How do we describe habitats?

- Why should we care about habitats?

- What do you know about habitats in your state?

Add your own questions!

Endangered Species

The number of plant and animal species threatened by extinction worldwide has been increasing dramatically in recent years due to many factors, such as growth in human population, loss of habitats, use of chemicals, and over-fishing and over-hunting. Loss of one species can have many known—and unknown—effects on other species. Helping students become aware of the issues surrounding endangered species is necessary preparation for the decisions they will make in their lifetimes.

Enduring Understandings

- Systems are composed of parts that interact with each other.

- Parts of an ecosystem are dependent on each other.

- Organisms share limited resources.

- Changes in environment can affect the survival of individuals and of species.

- Living organisms can contribute to the health of the environment.

- Human activities can have positive and negative effects on the environment.

Vocabulary List

- Captive bred
- Encroachment
- Extinct
- Pesticide

- Poach
- Pollution
- Predator
- Prey

- Protected animal
- Vanishing breed
- Vulnerable
- Wildlife

Essential Questions

Use these questions to help students pursue the topic of endangered species.

- What do living things need to survive?

- What is the relationship between living things and their environment?

- How do living things continue to adapt to changes in the environment?

- How are species interrelated?

- What causes a species to become extinct?

- How is the wide assortment of types of living things on Earth threatened?

- Why do some organisms survive and others don't?

- Why does it matter if a species disappears?

- How can humans and animals live together successfully?

- How are humans causing extinctions?

- Can we make a difference?

- How do you balance needs of humans with needs of other organisms?

Add your own questions!

Energy

The flow of energy drives all biological, chemical, physical, and geological systems on Earth. The transfer of energy into its many forms affects every facet of our lives. At the same time, the need for safe, clean energy sources and efficient uses of energy are global priorities that have the potential to capture students' interest and imagination.

Enduring Understandings

- The natural world is composed of matter and energy.

- There are regular, predictable patterns in the universe.

- Changes take place because of the transfer of energy.

- The sun can cause changes on Earth.

- Energy cannot be created or destroyed; the total energy of the universe remains constant.

- Humans have needs that are met through interactions with the environment.

Vocabulary List

- Chemical
- Force
- Fuel
- Heat
- Kinetic

- Light
- Magnetism
- Matter
- Motion
- Potential

- Sound
- Source
- Thermal
- Transfer
- Transformation

Essential Questions

Use these questions to help students investigate the many forms of energy at work in their lives.

- How do physical changes in our environment affect our lives?

- What role does chemistry play in our lives?

- Where do we find energy?

- How do we know if something has energy?

- How do we put the sun to work?

- How can the transfer of energy alter systems?

- How are forms of energy different or similar?

- How do all living things use energy?

- How are energy and the food chain related?

- How do humans rely on energy?

- How can humans control energy?

- What is energy efficiency?

Add your own questions!

Reading Fiction

From prehistoric times to the present era, stories have been created, shared, and enjoyed. A well-crafted story can provide entertainment, hold up a mirror to society, teach us about ourselves, and let us exercise our imaginations to travel anywhere in time and place. Providing students with tools they can use to explore and talk about their experiences reading fiction can help enrich their lives as readers and thinkers.

Enduring Understandings

- Fiction weaves together the elements of character, plot, and setting.

- Conflict is essential to fiction.

- Fiction explores characters' motives and actions as they deal with conflict.

- Fiction expresses universal truths about human experience.

- Literary elements work together to convey themes in fiction.

- Reading fiction can be a means of self-discovery.

Vocabulary List

- Character
- Climax
- Dialogue
- Falling action
- Mood

- Narrator
- Novel
- Plot
- Point of view
- Rising action

- Setting
- Style
- Theme

Essential Questions

Students can use these questions to guide their thinking about the works of fiction they are reading.

- How is fiction like life?

- Why do people create fiction?

- How does the author make the characters come to life?

- Why do main characters face problems?

- Why do characters change?

- How does conflict lead to change?

- How does the setting influence the characters and the plot?

- What characters do you relate to, and why?

- How do you figure out the theme?

- How does the author hook and hold the reader's attention?

- How does point of view affect the story?

- How would the story change if the narrator changed?

- How is style important to the telling of a story?

Historical Fiction

- In what ways may events in historical fiction connect to real history?

- How do authors of historical fiction make the time period and characters come alive?

- What types of insights about life in a given time period might an author provide?

- How do authors help us draw comparisons between life today and life in another period of time?

Fantasy

- How does life in the fantasy world help us learn about the real world?

- What kinds of conflicts typically occur in fantasy narratives?

- What is believable about the story?

Science Fiction

- How does the author use advances in science or technology to tell the story?

- Would you want to live in the world of this story? Why or why not?

- What message about life in the present time might the author be presenting?

Realistic Fiction

- How does the author make the story seem real?

- Are there any characters that you relate to in the story? Why or why not?

- What does the author want readers to remember about the story?

Mystery

- What role does suspense play in mysteries?

- What qualities make a mystery successful or unsuccessful?

Add your own questions!

Big Idea 23

Reading Nonfiction

Many of the topics students are most interested in exploring are found in nonfiction. Helping students engage with a wide variety of nonfiction writing can reap many benefits. Reading nonfiction can help students build background knowledge, increase vocabulary, build outside interests, and become more proficient readers of content across the curriculum. Interests developed through nonfiction reading can even lead to career choices.

Enduring Understandings

- Different types of texts have different purposes and structures.

- Nonfiction is written for a variety of purposes.

- Nonfiction texts have special features to help make the meaning clear.

- The writer of nonfiction chooses structures, graphics, and text features to suit the purpose and audience.

- Writers use different techniques in nonfiction to get across their meaning.

Vocabulary List

- Argument
- Author's purpose
- Cause/effect
- Chronological
- Compare/contrast

- Evidence
- Expository
- Fact
- Opinion
- Organization

- Paraphrase
- Persuasive
- Sentence structure
- Summary
- Text features

Essential Questions

Students can use these questions to guide their reading of the various types of nonfiction.

- Why do people write nonfiction?

- What are the characteristics of nonfiction?

- What are ways to identify a piece of writing as nonfiction?

- How is nonfiction different from fiction?

- How is reading nonfiction different from reading fiction?

- How is nonfiction like fiction?

- How does understanding the structure of the text help the reader understand the meaning?

- How does an author's purpose and audience influence decisions made while writing?

- How does the author's language match his or her purpose in writing?

- What questions are raised but not answered?

- What opinions of the author are expressed, and how easy are they to tell from facts?

- Why do people read nonfiction?

- Why is nonfiction an important genre of literature?

Biography/Autobiography/Memoir

- Why can you trust what the author says about the person being written about?

- What opinion about the person does the author seem to express, and why do you agree or disagree with that opinion?

- What information is left out, and why?

- Why is the person's life worth reading about?

Persuasive Nonfiction

- What techniques does the author use to get the reader on his or her side?

- How does the author use evidence and research to support the arguments?

- How persuasive are the arguments the author makes?

- Why might people react differently to the author's ideas?

- Why is being a careful reader of persuasive writing a valuable life skill?

Informative Essay/Magazine Article/Newspaper Article

- What does the author want the reader to learn?

- How does the author organize the information and make it easy to follow?

- How do you know if the information is trustworthy?

- How do you know if the information is up to date?

- What techniques does the author use to make the reading interesting?

- What would you like to ask the author?

Add your own questions!

Reading Poetry

To immerse students in the genre of poetry is to expose them to language and imagination at their best. Poetry is a celebration of the magic, power, and beauty of words. The more poems students read and the more varieties of poems they are exposed to, the more likely they are to come to understand and appreciate the value that poetry can add to their own lives.

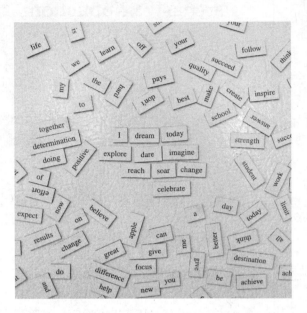

Enduring Understandings

- Language can be used to express thoughts and feelings.

- Poetry expresses ideas and feelings in compact, imaginative, and musical language.

- Some poems are serious, while others can be funny.

- In poetry, words can have layers and shades of meaning.

- Poetry is meant to be read aloud.

- Understanding how a poem works helps us appreciate its message.

Vocabulary List

- Alliteration
- Figurative language
- Imagery
- Metaphor
- Meter

- Narrative poetry
- Onomatopoeia
- Repetition
- Rhyme
- Rhyme scheme

- Rhythm
- Simile
- Stanza

Essential Questions

Students can use these questions to become more proficient readers of the genre of poetry.

- What makes a piece of writing a poem?

- How is poetry different from fiction and from nonfiction?

- Why do people write poetry?

- Why do people read poetry?

- How are feelings expressed in poems?

- Why is reading poetry aloud so important?

- How does a reader figure out the meaning of a poem?

- How does a poet paint a picture with words?

- How does a poet appeal to all the senses?

- How does the shape or form of a poem affect the meaning?

- What makes a poem great?

- What is the relationship between the poem and the poet?

Add your own questions!

Big Idea 25

Facing Challenges

Conflict is key to literature, so the big idea "Facing Challenges" is ideal for immersing students in the conflicts and challenges played out in the stories they read. The wide range of literature revolving around challenges allows students to connect past to present and near to far. Discussing approaches and reactions to challenges is also an excellent way to tap into students' own experiences and provides insight into the conflicts faced by people around the world.

Enduring Understandings

- Everyone faces his or her own unique set of challenges.

- Being able to face and overcome challenges is a valuable trait in life.

- It takes hard work to overcome challenges.

- People help each other to face challenges.

- Overcoming challenges sometimes requires thinking in new ways.

- Understanding what cannot be changed is part of facing challenges.

Vocabulary List

- Adaptable
- Confront
- Defiant
- Endurance
- Grapple

- Incite
- Inspiration
- Persistence
- Resolute
- Resourceful

- Steadfast
- Strategy
- Survivor

Essential Questions

Use these questions to help students explore the many facets of facing challenges.

- What does it mean to face a challenge?

- What kinds of challenges are often faced by individuals?

- What are the types of challenges that a country might face?

- What kinds of challenges are faced by people all around the world?

- What steps must be taken to face a challenge?

- What obstacles within a person can get in the way of meeting a challenge?

- What are the advantages of facing challenges that involve others?

- What does it take to overcome challenges?

- How can nature cause challenges?

- Is a challenge ever too hard to overcome?

- How can literature help us learn to face challenges?

Add your own questions!

Heroes

The debate over who is or is not a hero is timeless in literature as well as in life. Opportunities to encounter an array of heroes, from all walks of life and from many cultures and time periods, can help students gain valuable insights into human behavior. Each encounter can help students develop their own criteria for measuring a hero's worth.

Enduring Understandings

- Heroes face challenges in particular times and situations.

- Heroes are defined by their deeds and choices.

- Qualities considered heroic can change over time.

- Cultural values can influence what is considered heroic.

- Heroes help meet the needs of society.

- Heroes make a difference in the lives of others.

- A hero's values and beliefs can influence others.

- The potential to be a hero exists in everyone.

Vocabulary List

- Accomplishment
- Adversary
- Champion
- Chivalrous
- Coward

- Crisis
- Exploit
- Fortitude
- Gallant
- Liberate

- Oppression
- Tireless
- Valiant
- Villain

Essential Questions

Use these questions to guide student exploration about the concept of heroes.

- What does it take to be a hero?

- What kinds of heroes are there?

- How do heroes face challenges?

- Do people choose to become heroes?

- How are heroes in the past the same as or different from heroes today?

- How are heroes in stories the same as or different from heroes in real life?

- How do heroes affect the people around them?

- Is a hero always perfect?

- What is the opposite of a hero?

- Are some heroes more heroic than others?

- Why are there so many stories about heroes?

- What acts do you consider heroic?

Add your own questions!

Big Idea 27

Friendships

Whether real, imaginary, human, or animal, friends are at the center of students' lives. Literature abounds in lessons about the rewards and pains of friendship. Every student can enter the conversation about friendship with prior knowledge to draw from.

Enduring Understandings

- Friends are a key part of a healthy life.

- Friends lend support in trying times.

- Friendships can develop unexpectedly in unlikely ways and places.

- Conflicts can happen in relationships.

- It is sometimes hard to recognize who true friends are.

- Friendship is based on respect.

- Friends can be honest with each other.

Vocabulary List

- Affinity
- Allegiance
- Attentive
- Clique
- Confide
- Cooperation
- Esteem
- Inseparable
- Loyalty
- Peer
- Similar
- Sympathetic
- Trustworthy
- Unconditional

Essential Questions

Use these questions to enrich the discussion of friendship.

- What does it take to be a good friend?

- What kinds of friends are there?

- How do people become good friends?

- What do friends do for each other?

- What are the benefits of having a good friend?

- In what ways should friends be alike or act alike?

- How do we make and keep friends?

- How do we know who our friends really are?

- Why is it sometimes hard to make friends?

- What can cause friendships to change?

- How do friends solve conflicts?

- How can differences or disagreements strengthen friendships?

Add your own questions!

Big Idea 28

Finding Courage

Literature and history are full of tales of people finding courage. These stories range from single dramatic deeds to long-term accomplishments. The many facets of courage include bravery, perseverance, integrity, and passion. Understanding that courage can mean much more than a single act of heroism is an important life lesson.

Enduring Understandings

- Courage is shown in different ways in different situations.

- Courage is not always visible to others.

- Courage can be learned.

- A person can be afraid and still face obstacles with courage.

- A single person's act of courage can affect the lives of many.

- Learning about courage in others can inspire someone to be courageous.

Vocabulary List

- Attitude
- Challenge
- Circumstance
- Cope
- Endeavor

- Feat
- Ominous
- Peril
- Resolve
- Stamina

- Survival
- Treacherous
- Unwavering
- Valor

Essential Questions

Use these questions to help students develop a fuller understanding of the many dimensions of courage.

- What does it mean to show courage?

- What are different types of courage?

- How can an act of courage affect others?

- What kinds of situations call for courage?

- Where does courage come from?

- What does it mean to have the "courage of your convictions"?

- Can someone be afraid and courageous at the same time?

- What are some ways people show courage?

- What is the opposite of courage?

- Why is courage valued?

- How are risk-taking and courage related?

- How are endurance and courage related?

Add your own questions!

Big Idea 29

Family Heritage

Families inherit a wealth of stories, traditions, histories, behaviors, and attitudes rooted in the past. Learning to appreciate, celebrate, learn from, continue, and build on this heritage is the challenge of each generation. Both fiction and nonfiction are ideal for focusing student discussion on the rich and often complex concept of family heritage.

Enduring Understandings

- People and events from the past affect the present and the future.

- A family's history, traditions, celebrations, and daily patterns of life make up its heritage.

- Some aspects of a family's heritage are unique, and some are common to other families.

- A family's traditions and customs may change over time.

- Family heritage can be reflected in fine art forms and in artifacts.

- People learn about themselves when they learn about their family heritage.

Vocabulary List

- Ancestor
- Culture
- Custom
- Descendant

- Ethnic
- Generation
- Identity
- Keepsake

- Legacy
- Nationality
- Observance
- Oral

Essential Questions

Use these questions to generate thinking about family heritage.

- What is family heritage?

- How does family heritage affect one's beliefs and behaviors?

- How do families share their history?

- Why do families pass down stories?

- How can people benefit from knowing their family history?

- Why are family traditions important?

- Why do different families have different traditions?

- Why is it important to appreciate our own heritage?

- How do families and individuals honor their own heritage?

- How do people honor other families' heritage?

- What can be gained by learning about the heritage of families from many different countries?

- How can learning about our family heritage help us learn about ourselves?

Add your own questions!

Big Idea 30

Nature—Friend or Foe?

The range of physical environments and living creatures we call nature holds endless fascination for students. The same wide variety of elements of the natural world can be found in the plots, settings, and characters in literature. In each case, students will discover that the encounters between humans and the natural world can range from deadly conflict to peaceful coexistence.

 ## Enduring Understandings

- Humans depend on resources in nature to meet their basic needs.

- Nature sometimes affects humans in negative ways.

- Humans often try to channel nature for their own use.

- People are inspired by elements of nature to produce a variety of artistic creations.

- Characters' quests for survival against forces in nature are common in literature.

Vocabulary List

- Appreciate
- Destruction
- Ecology
- Environment
- Hostile

- Intimidating
- Majestic
- Nurturing
- Preservation
- Prevail

- Scenery
- Survival
- Sustainable
- Violent

Essential Questions

Use these questions to explore the wide range of experiences people can have with the natural world.

- In what ways can nature be enjoyed by people?

- In what ways can nature seem like an enemy?

- How do people show respect for nature?

- How has nature inspired various types of artists?

- What responsibilities do people have to nature?

- In what way is nature mysterious?

- How and what can people learn from nature?

- What does it take to survive in nature?

- What does it mean to be in tune with nature?

- In what ways do people underestimate nature?

- What should the relationship between humans and animals be?

Add your own questions!

Teamwork

Collaboration, mutual respect, appreciation of diversity—these are some of the hallmarks of successful teamwork. Literature provides countless examples of characters facing the challenges of working as a team to reach a common goal. From their own experiences at home, at school, and at play, students have already come to know firsthand the value and challenges of working together. Teamwork continues to play an important role throughout the grades and on into the workplace.

Enduring Understandings

- People work together to get things done.

- Team members share common goals.

- Interactions between people can lead to conflict.

- Every member of a team contributes to the team's success.

- Members of successful teams trust and respect one another.

Vocabulary List

- Achievement
- Assistance
- Collaborate
- Compromise
- Constructive

- Cooperate
- Effort
- Goal
- Interpersonal
- Involvement

- Mutual
- Problem-solving
- Support

Essential Questions

Use these questions to direct students in an exploration of the concept of teamwork.

- What are the advantages of working as a team?

- What are the disadvantages of working as a team?

- How do individuals contribute to the success of a team?

- What are the qualities of an effective team?

- What challenges can teams face?

- How do teams settle conflicts?

- Do all teams need leaders?

- How might a team improve over time?

- How might a team be less successful over time?

- What keeps team members from trying their best?

- How does an ordinary team become a "dream team"?

- Why does teamwork sometimes fail?

Add your own questions!

Mathematical Operations

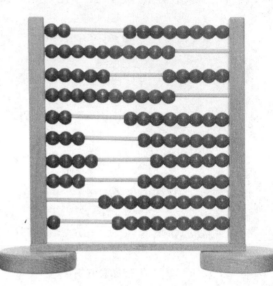

Helping students develop both conceptual understanding and fluency in mathematical operations is a key part of the mathematics curriculum in the upper elementary grades. A firm grounding in the big picture of how addition, subtraction, multiplication, and division interrelate and how they are vital tools in life can help students build the positive attitudes that will help them become confident, efficient, and effective problem-solvers.

Enduring Understandings

- Mathematics is a system for organizing the world quantitatively.

- Numbers can be manipulated according to standardized rules.

- Operations with numbers are used to solve problems at all levels of math.

- Every numerical operation has an inverse.

- There can be more than one effective way to solve a problem.

- Computation and fluency in operations are vital life skills.

Vocabulary List

- Addition
- Computation
- Difference
- Dividend
- Division

- Divisor
- Fluency
- Inverse
- Multiplication
- Product

- Quotient
- Remainder
- Subtraction
- Sum

Essential Questions

Use these questions to help students build a conceptual understanding of mathematical operations.

- How can math help us make sense of the world around us?

- How can numbers be manipulated?

- How can we show how numbers are related to each other?

- How are mathematical operations (addition, subtraction, multiplication, division) related to each other?

- Why do we need mathematical operations?

- Why are mathematical rules necessary?

- What makes a strategy for working with numbers efficient and effective?

- Why is order of operations important?

- Why is it important to know what operation to use in different situations?

- How does reasoning relate to mathematical operations?

- Why is fluency in computing important in life?

Add your own questions!

Big Idea 33

Fractions and Decimals

Fractions often present a stumbling block for students. At the same time, students come to the topic with a clear understanding of what it means to share half of something with a friend. Beginning with their own experiences, students can build conceptual knowledge of how to relate numbers, how to divide a whole, how to manipulate fractions and decimals, and how to express and picture the same quantities in a variety of ways.

Enduring Understandings

- Mathematics provides a variety of ways to express relationships between numbers.

- Numbers can be expressed in different forms, ordered, and compared.

- Wholes can be divided into parts.

- Fractions and decimals express a relationship between two numbers.

- Different numbers can have the same value.

Vocabulary List

- Decimal
- Decimal point
- Denominator
- Equivalent
- Improper fraction

- Mixed number
- Number line
- Numerator
- Percent
- Place value

- Proper fraction
- Proportion
- Ratio
- Whole number

Essential Questions

Use these questions to provide students with a deeper understanding of fractions and decimals.

- When is it helpful to break things into parts?

- How do we show relationships between numbers?

- Why is it useful to compare numbers?

- How can we prove that numbers are both the same and different?

- How can pictures help us see how numbers are related?

- How are fractions and decimals alike and different?

- How are fractions and decimals parts of a whole?

- How are fractions and decimals used in real-world situations?

- How do mathematical operations relate to fractions and decimals?

- When are fractions and whole numbers used together in real life?

- What are the advantages of fractions? What are the advantages of decimals?

- How can understanding fractions and decimals make life easier?

Add your own questions!

Big Idea 34

Estimation

Many real-life applications of math do not require exact answers. Instead, knowledgeable people rely on estimations, their educated predictions of quantities or of the outcomes of computations. The practical value of estimating in real-world situations has caused the skill to gain in prominence and importance as a big idea in math. It is also an important strategy for judging the reasonableness of an answer and for catching errors made when using calculators.

Enduring Understandings

- Math is useful in everyday life.

- Problems can be solved in more than one way.

- Estimations produce approximate results.

- In some situations, an estimate can be as useful as an exact answer.

- Estimation is useful for judging the reasonableness of an answer.

Vocabulary List

- Approximately
- Benchmark number
- Calculate
- Clustering strategy
- Compatible numbers
- Estimate

- Even number
- Exact
- Front-end estimating
- Justify
- Mental math
- Overestimate

- Reasonable
- Reasoning
- Rounding
- Underestimate

Essential Questions

Use these questions as you encourage students to deepen their understanding of the role of estimating.

- How can patterns help us solve problems?

- When do people estimate in real life?

- What is the difference between guessing and estimating?

- How do people make good estimations in math?

- Why should answers in math make sense?

- When is an estimate more appropriate than an exact calculation?

- What makes an estimate reasonable?

- What makes an answer exact?

- How important are estimations in real life?

- How do we get better at estimating?

- When is overestimating or underestimating a problem?

- What are advantages and disadvantages of estimating?

Add your own questions!

Measurement

One important facet of mathematics is our standard systems of measurement. An accurate and consistent system of measurement is more than useful; it is a foundation of our economy and a necessity for international interaction. Without a consistent system of measurement, local and international trade would become chaotic. Systems of measurement facilitate communication in all aspects of human life.

Enduring Understandings

- Objects have specific features that can expressed in numbers.

- Measurement helps us understand and describe our world.

- Objects can be compared using the same attribute.

- Measurements can be made with appropriate tools, techniques, and formulas.

- Standard units of measurement provide common language for communicating.

- Context helps us decide the appropriate degree of accuracy in measurement.

Vocabulary List

- Accurate
- Capacity
- Convert
- Dimension
- Distance
- Length
- Metric system
- Perimeter
- Precision
- Standard
- Unit
- Volume
- Weigh
- Width

Essential Questions

Use these questions to help students explore the mathematical thinking behind the very practical subject of measurement.

- What types of things can be measured?

- How can something be measured?

- Why is measurement important?

- Why can we describe measurement as a system?

- Why do measurements need both numbers and units?

- Why do we need standard units of measurement?

- Why do we convert units of measurement?

- How precise must measurement be?

- How do measurements help us compare objects?

- What types of problems are solved with measurements?

- How do we choose the best unit of measurement to use?

- How can there be more than one way to measure something?

- How do we measure when we don't have a standard tool?

Add your own questions!

Patterns

Patterns are everywhere. Scientific and artistic tasks often revolve around finding patterns in nature. The concept of patterns is so prevalent in mathematics that it has been called "the science of patterns." Major principles in algebra and geometry can be formulated as generalizations of patterns in numbers and shapes. Students will build a strong foundation of algebra readiness by recognizing, analyzing, and constructing patterns in a variety of contexts in the math classroom.

Enduring Understandings

- Order exists in the universe.

- Attributes of objects can be sorted by a pattern unit and can be extended.

- Patterns have rules and relationships.

- Some things change in consistent patterns and some things change in changing patterns.

- Algebra provides the language for communicating patterns in mathematics.

- Patterns are useful tools for making predictions.

Vocabulary List

- Algebraic thinking
- Configuration
- Consistent
- Describe
- Extend

- Fractal
- Generalize
- Generate
- Order
- Random

- Recursive
- Relationship
- Repeating
- Represent
- Sequence

Essential Questions

Use these questions to help students build on their knowledge of patterns.

- Where in the real world do we find patterns?

- What are different ways to represent patterns?

- How do we figure out and describe patterns?

- How are patterns used to make discoveries about our universe and about ourselves?

- How are patterns used to communicate in math?

- How can change be represented mathematically?

- How is math used to design patterns?

- Why is math sometimes called "the science of patterns"?

- How can patterns be organized?

- How can we use patterns to show a relationship?

- How do patterns help us compare and contrast?

- How can patterns help in making predictions?

- How can change be represented mathematically?

Add your own questions!

Geometric Shapes

From art to architecture, geometric shapes play essential roles in everyday life. Learning the mathematical principles that go into creating, describing, classifying, and manipulating shapes can open up new worlds to students. Working with geometric shapes and seeing the possible results can demonstrate to them that studying spatial relationships is not an abstract math activity but an essential life skill.

Enduring Understandings

- Geometry is a representation of the world around us.

- Geometric shapes exist in the natural and the man-made world.

- Objects can be analyzed, sorted, and compared by attributes.

- Knowing about shapes helps us solve problems and make sense of the world.

- The properties of a geometric figure determine its use.

- Shapes can be combined to make new shapes.

- Manipulation of geometric shapes can be a useful tool in real life.

Vocabulary List

- Angle
- Congruent
- Cube
- Cylinder
- Line segment
- Parallelogram
- Plane
- Point
- Polygon
- Quadrilateral
- Rhombus
- Spatial
- Three-dimensional
- Trapezoid

Essential Questions

Use these questions to help students connect principles of geometry to the physical shapes that make up their world.

- How do we use geometry to make sense of the real world?

- Where in the real world are there geometric shapes?

- What are the ways to describe shapes?

- Why do similarities and differences exist between geometric shapes?

- How can objects be compared using descriptors from geometry?

- Why is it important to be able to describe and name geometric shapes?

- How are geometric shapes constructed?

- What is the relationship between the shape of an object and its use?

- How do geometric shapes help us solve problems and make sense of the world?

- What is the relationship between plane states and solid states?

- How can putting shapes together and taking them apart help us understand them?

- Can any geometric shape be transformed into any other shape? Why or why not?

Add your own questions!

Big Idea 38

Money

Principles of counting, operations, fractions, decimals, and measurement all converge and get put to practical use when it comes to money. Learning how to earn, save, and spend money holds great interest for students, and the mystique connected to money can lead them to wide ranges of explorations—from the use of money throughout history to an interest in foreign cultures to a deepening appreciation of math.

Enduring Understandings

- Mathematics is useful in everyday life.

- All pieces of money have a specific, definite value.

- There is a relationship between units of money in our society.

- Different combinations of money may make the same amount.

- Money can be used to buy things.

- Currency can be represented and compared as fractional parts.

Vocabulary List

- Calculate
- Cash
- Change
- Conversion
- Cost

- Currency
- Dime
- Dollar
- Dollar sign
- Expense

- Finance
- Loan
- Nickel
- Owe
- Penny

- Price
- Profit
- Purchase
- Quarter
- Total

Essential Questions

Use these questions to capitalize on prior knowledge and interest in the subject of money.

- In what ways can units of money be grouped?

- How do units in a system relate to each other?

- How can counting help us make sense of the world around us?

- Why do we have money?

- Why is it important to understand the value of coins?

- Why do we need consistent, standard values for coins?

- Why is it important to represent amounts of money in different ways?

- How does money relate to patterns?

- How does understanding numerical operations help us use money?

- Why do different countries have different kinds of money?

- How do people with different monetary systems exchange goods and services?

- What is the relationship between fractions and money?

- When is it useful to estimate amounts of money?

Add your own questions!

Data and Statistics

Working with data and statistics provides the opportunity for students to understand that mathematics is sensible, useful, and worthwhile. Manipulating and displaying data calls on students to draw from and apply their knowledge in the areas of reasoning, modeling, working with patterns, precise calculating, problem solving, and communicating. In turn, data and statistics help us explain and predict events in our daily lives.

Enduring Understandings

- Math helps us see patterns.

- Organization of information shows relationships.

- Data can be collected, organized, sorted, and analyzed in a variety of ways.

- Data helps us make sense of information in our world.

- Predictions can often be expressed and justified through the use of data.

- Communicating information is critical in real-life situations.

Vocabulary List

- Average
- Bar graph
- Chart
- Circle graph
- Distribution
- Frequency
- Graph
- Histogram
- Line graph
- Matrix
- Mean
- Median
- Mode
- Outlier
- Probability
- Range
- Trend

Essential Questions

Use these questions to help students gain a better understanding about the importance of data and statistics.

- Why is math valuable?

- Why and how do we sort information?

- When is it necessary to communicate and justify information?

- Why do we analyze data?

- Why is finding patterns useful?

- What are some ways we can organize data?

- What kinds of problems can be solved with data analysis?

- When is it helpful to collect more than one set of data?

- Why and how can we represent the same data in a variety of ways?

- How can graphic representation of data help solve problems?

- How do people use data and statistics to influence others?

- How do data and statistics help us make predictions?

- Why would we want to know how likely it is that an event might occur?

Add your own questions!

Algebra

There is no better environment than algebra for learning and developing problem-solving skills. In every situation, students must analyze what they do and don't know about a problem, determine a method for finding a solution, and then check the results to see if their choices were accurate. To teach algebra is to provide students with a powerful toolkit for dealing with real-world situations in a systematic, analytic manner.

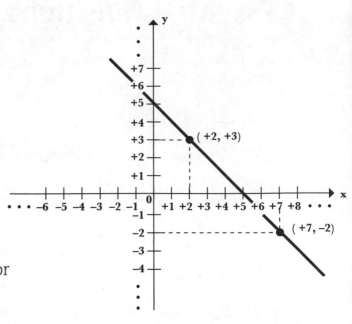

Enduring Understandings

- Algebra is the foundation for other mathematics and sciences.

- Logical reasoning can be used to help us approach and analyze a problem, explain our processes, and check answers.

- Symbols, such as numbers and variables, can be used to represent real-life quantities and relationships.

- Equations are tools for problem solving and for expressing ideas, concepts, and relationships.

- Graphs and charts are visual representations of functions and numerical relationships.

Vocabulary List

- Algebraic expressions
- Analyze
- Compute
- Data
- Domain
- Equation

- Exponents
- Factor
- Function
- Operations
- Patterns
- Proportion

- Ratio
- Symbol
- System
- Value
- Variable

Essential Questions

Use these questions to help students gain a better understanding about the importance of algebra in the real world.

- How can we use algebra to solve real-world problems?

- What tools or skills are needed to effectively compute with numbers?

- What is a mathematical system?

- How do we choose the best method for solving an equation?

- How can we solve for the unknown?

- How can verbal statements be changed into algebraic expressions?

- What are variables, and what can they represent?

- How do we analyze and understand patterns, relations, and functions?

- When can graphs and tables be used to represent relationships?

- What does a function look like?

- How do we know where to begin solving a problem?

- Why is it important to know the order of operations?

- How do I decide which strategy to use when solving a problem?

Add your own questions!

Big Idea: Heroes

Applications in Literature

Exploring the idea of a hero in literature is natural for students who have already been exposed to many different types of heroes in print and other media. Building from these exposures, students can deepen their understandings by looking at a wide variety of heroic characters, from those in epics to those in modern realistic fiction. They can also appreciate and evaluate the techniques authors use to bring heroes to life. Students may use the questions on page 61, as well as the following, to examine the patterns and possibilities of heroes and heroic actions in literature.

- Why are there heroes in stories from every age and every culture?
- What patterns are there in stories with heroes?
- How do writers make characters heroic?
- How can heroes in literature reflect the values of the times?

My Essential Questions

Applications in Social Studies

Heroes are shaped by their societies, and they in turn shape their societies. Allow students to use these questions to delve into the role of real-life heroes in history.

- How can a hero represent a culture?
- What is the same and different about all heroes?
- Why can there be disagreement about who is a hero in history?
- What does it mean to be an unsung hero, and what are examples in history?
- What is the relationship between a hero and a leader?
- How do people honor heroes?

My Essential Questions

Applications in Fine Arts

Heroic deeds have always inspired great works of art. These works are products of individuals and their culture and provide us with an opportunity to examine the values of an era. Use these questions to help students investigate the depiction and celebration of heroes through the arts.

- How do people use art and music to celebrate heroes?
- How do artists express admiration for someone?
- Why is it important to honor heroes in works of art?
- How do artists' cultures influence how they depict and honor heroes?
- Why is it valuable to study images of heroes across time in art?
- How might celebrations of heroes in the arts change in the future?

My Essential Questions

Applications in Science

The field of science is filled with men and women who have exhibited the qualities of heroism while braving new frontiers of learning and asking difficult questions about our world and the universe. Students can use these questions to apply their thinking about heroes to the work of scientists.

- How can the field of science have heroes?
- Who are examples of heroes in science?
- Are there heroes in science besides scientists? If so, who and why?
- Why might there be disagreements about heroics in science?
- What do heroes in science have in common with any other heroes?
- Who might be future heroes in science?

My Essential Questions

Big Idea: Planet Earth

Applications in Geography

Studying Earth's geography allows students to connect and better understand ideas from science, social studies, and literature. Use these questions to help students see how the geography of Earth impacts its people.

- How is Earth an integrated system?
- How and why are patterns of physical features different across Earth?
- How are places on Earth alike and different?
- How does geography influence human behavior?
- What is the relationship between cultures and geography?
- Why is the study of Earth's geography useful?

My Essential Questions

Applications in Language Arts

An essential part of any story is setting, the time and place that it occurs on Earth. As Eudora Welty commented, "Every story would be another story, and unrecognizable as art, if it took up its characters and plot and happened somewhere else." Students can use these questions to explore setting in fiction.

- What does it mean to say a character is "from somewhere"?
- What decisions does a fiction writer have to make about setting in a story?
- How does setting contribute to the mood of a story?
- How can a story's setting influence its plot?
- What is the importance of setting in historical fiction?

My Essential Questions

Applications in Visual Arts

Artists have always been inspired by the natural scenery of their home planet. They produce works that reflect moods, perspectives, and interpretations of what they see on Earth. Use these questions to help students connect the visual arts to the natural world around them.

- How do artists express ideas and feelings about Earth?
- How do artists' renderings of scenes on Earth relate to the real places?
- How do artists and photographers look at places on Earth in the same ways and in different ways?
- How does the culture of the artist influence his or her creations?

My Essential Questions

Applications in Mathematics

Many of Earth's features can be studied and described through mathematics. From weather and climate to measurements and the telling of time, math is at work whenever Earth is the topic of study. Use these questions to let students come to realize the value of mathematics in getting to know their home planet.

- How do scientists use math to study the planet Earth?
- How does math help us understand physical features of Earth?
- What do we measure on Earth, and why?
- How do we use math to make predictions about Earth?

My Essential Questions

Big Idea: Civil Rights Movement

Applications in Social Studies

The Civil Rights movement was a transforming time and continues to have effects worldwide. Rosa Parks and Martin Luther King, Jr., inspired efforts that pushed America to guarantee all citizens equal rights. Use these questions to deepen students' understanding of this critical time in history.

- Why and how do people struggle for social justice?
- What happens when people are denied civil rights?
- How can one person make a difference?
- What can we learn from the Civil Rights movement?
- Has the Civil Rights movement ended?

My Essential Questions

Applications in Language Arts

Literature has the power to make history come to life. The Civil Rights movement has inspired and continues to be the inspiration for poetry, fiction, drama, and other literature. Use these questions to help prepare students for reading literature about the Civil Rights movement.

- Why do writers continue to write about the Civil Rights movement?
- How does literature become a part of history?
- Why are speeches studied in both literature and social studies?

My Essential Questions

Applications in Visual Arts

Using a variety of visual media, artists have portrayed the heroic efforts of African Americans fighting for civil rights. Use these questions to guide students' exploration of the art and photography of the Civil Rights movement.

- How is art a mirror to life?
- How can photography affect history?
- How can something be both a cause and an effect?
- How does the Civil Rights movement continue to inspire artists today?

My Essential Questions

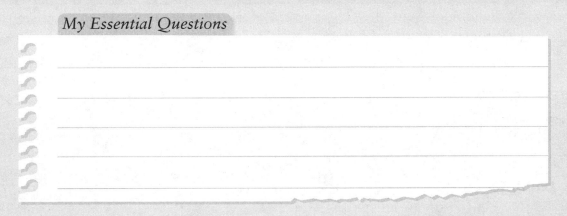

Applications in Music

The Civil Rights movement had a close connection to music. Across America, gospel, folk, blues, and jazz musicians lent their talents to the protest movement. By exploring these questions, students can begin to appreciate the powerful effects of the music that is now part of our national heritage.

- How do people communicate through music?
- How do music and history influence each other?
- How does music affect emotions?
- What inspires someone to create music?

My Essential Questions

Integrated Unit EQ Planner

Unit of study: _____

Dates: _____

Final project due/Assessment date: _____

Content-Area Applications

☐ **Arts**

EQs: _____

_____

☐ **Language Arts**

EQs: _____

_____

☐ **Geography**

EQs: _____

_____

☐ **Math**

EQs: _____

_____

☐ **Science**

EQs: _____

_____

☐ **Social Studies**

EQs: _____

_____

☐ **Other:** _____

EQs: _____

_____